This B  **f:**

(As You Wish To Be Known In The Oxford Club)

This book is not intended for general circulation. You are being asked, as a gentleman of honor, to hold the information in these pages in the strictest of confidence.

"Some men can make funny faces, others can make fools of themselves, others can make money."

— *Bernard Baruch*

In the Bill Of Rights, is there any mention of a man's right to wealth?

Does that document say you have an inalienable right to multiply your wealth and protect it from taxation? Inflation? Litigation? All forms of confiscation?

We think not.

The active pursuit and protection of wealth becomes a right only when you make it so. That is the essential truth of our times . . . and it is the purpose of this book.

You are about to sit in on a confidential fireside briefing with the Oxford Club founders.

These are men who've made wealth a constant companion, an inalienable right. Men who have an uncanny knack for uncovering small OTC stocks that rocket from $.77 to $12.53 in a single year. (See how they do it on page 57.)

These men have agreed to open their doors and share their insights and understandings with you . . . because you have shown yourself worthy of the Oxford Club.

Prepare now to join the founders around the fireplace at the 200-year old Ruttledge House in

Cornwall, England. These founders, in the order that you will meet them, are James Boxley Cooke, William Ruttledge, and Joseph Breckinridge.

Let the briefing begin.

CONTENTS

The dollar has lost 85% of its value in your lifetime. How much more will it lose before you act?

Why settle for a cat food retirement when people in your same position are upgrading to caviar?

New computer programs allow scientists to select winning investments with 80% accuracy. Ever done that well?

Invest in today's blue chips for *good* profits; invest in the breakthrough blue chips of tomorrow for *grand* profits (like our 1,500% grand slam of '94).

Looking to ride the new wave in real estate? Or move to tomorrow's choicest retirement haven? Look no further.

AMERICAN THE BEATEN-UP

JAMES COOKE

Let's begin at the beginning — *I love America!* It's my home. It has given me everything I have today. I have seen it through several wars, scandals, setbacks, and through it all, I've never stopped believing in America. I would gladly stand up and fight for her again today. But what would I be fighting for? What has America become? Sometimes I'm not so sure I know . . .

It doesn't seem so long ago that kids could play kick-the-can in the streets until well after dark . . . and no one worried.

I can remember taking a drive into the city for a day in the park or to take in a musical. Now I'm met with potholed streets, moral filth, and crazies running loose.

I can also remember when I worked proudly for a hard day's pay and a dollar stretched a long way. Now it seems that everyone's whining or complaining or sitting on their butts expecting a handout. They're all trying to get their hands on the money that a few of us have worked a lifetime to obtain.

Lawyers will sue us for it. The government

will tax it away from us. Some punk will take it right out of our pocket.

Perhaps I've grown nostalgic for the good old days, but from where I sit, "America the Beautiful" has become "America the Beaten-Up." And it has me worried. You and I have become the targets of envy in an envy-driven culture. There are great threats looming over our heads.

JOSEPH BRECKINRIDGE
It is these threats, and a profound sense that our world had changed dramatically, that prompted us to first meet, twenty years ago. As men, we had been educated at fine schools. We had done well in business and in our investments. But, quite frankly, we knew that more would be required.

If we hoped to succeed and rise above the mediocrity we saw all around us, we would have to join forces with like-minded men . . . and create the tools and strategies for securing and protecting great quantities of wealth.

We had to assert our right to wealth.

Toward that end, we founded the Oxford Club. We have since conducted our business in complete secrecy, adhering to a Code of Confidentiality that has helped us prosper on a grand scale.

William Ruttledge

You may be wondering, "Why me? Why am I receiving this private briefing?" The answer is simple, really.

We have it from a reliable source that you share our concerns. You are worried about the direction this country is headed. You feel the threats to your ability to cultivate wealth. And you have a great many experiences and insights which you can bring to the Club . . . enriching us all.

This notion of "mutual protection" is dear to us. It is our lodestar, our guiding principle.

And to turn this principle into a reality, we have over the years developed a vast resource base that virtually guarantees a man nine levels of wealth:

Buying Power
Luxury Retirement
Perfect Knowledge
Grand Profits
Private Property
Tax-Free Living
Asset Protection
Complete Privacy
Safe Harbor

Our purpose and very reason for being is to secure these rights for our Members. We have no

other agenda. No other allegiances or affilia-
tions. Our purpose is singular: To marshall the
talents of a global network of business and
investment specialists for our Members' benefit.

Let's cut to the chase, then. Here's how it
happens:

Phase 1 — Move Onto Secure Ground

Phase 2 — Lead To Your Strength

Phase 3 — Never Ever Accept Losses

This three-phase strategy has been used by
thousands of Club members to multiply wealth,
master every situation, and prosper on a grand
scale. We now invite you to learn more.

Chapter One

A MAN'S RIGHT TO BUYING POWER

The dollar has lost 85% of its value in your lifetime. How much more will it lose before you act?

JOSEPH

All the charts and statistics and sworn testimony before Congress don't say as much about your loss of buying power as this one story.

It goes back to 1970. I'd been teaching at the University since '63. I got my tenure that year which meant a raise in salary. I wanted to put the money into something worthwhile, so I decided to take advantage of some GI Bill benefits from my time in the Korean War. Real estate, I thought. Definitely real estate.

So, there I was, standing in front of a piece of real estate in Sundance, Utah. It was a great piece of property on a crystal blue trout stream. I wanted that place. Wanted it bad. I figured it could be my little piece of heaven far removed from the anti-war turmoil that had engulfed America.

At the same time that I was looking at the

property, so was a Japanese businessman. We both knew that Robert Redford was setting up a Film Institute there, and that land values would soon skyrocket. Unfortunately, the property was listed for $100,000 and neither of us could afford it.

Locked out of buying land in your own country.

Time passed. I've made money, so have a lot of Japanese businessmen. Last year I went back to look at other property in Sundance, and coincidentally, so did a Japanese businessman. A similar parcel was now listed for $300,000. While I can afford it now, to me, it's no bargain. I passed on it, and chose to look elsewhere. To the Japanese businessman, however, it was a whole 'nother thing.

You see, back in 1970, when the asking price was $100,000, the Japanese businessman would have had to pony up 35 million yen to buy it. That was the exchange rate at the time. But 25 years later, things are quite different. Although the price for me is $300,000—triple the former asking price, the Japanese man has to pay only 30 million yen. That's the new exchange rate—even after all the destruction and financial hardship of the Kobe earthquake. The price hasn't tripled for him, it has fallen by almost 15%. He has no trouble buying it!

JAMES

Yes, the dollar used to be the envy of the world. It's power was unstoppable. But that's all history. Now we look out across the waters and see that it's the deutschmark, the Swiss franc, and the yen that rule. That gives these countries a tremendous advantage over us. They enjoy the buying power that we used to enjoy.

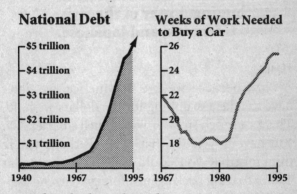

What do these charts have in common?

WILLIAM

Another example of our loss of buying power is the number of paychecks it takes for us to buy a mid-size car. Twenty years ago, it took the average American worker 17-1/2 week's worth of paychecks to be able to buy a Ford Mustang. Today, a new

Mustang costs 26 weeks of work. The average worker spends two more months on the job to buy the same thing as he could have bought 25 years ago.

JOSEPH

In the old days, we could have put that two months of income into savings and investments, preparing for the future. But those days are gone.

You can again enjoy the buying power of the Swiss, Germans, and Japanese.

JAMES

Just because we live in America, we don't have to take a drubbing for the dollars we hold. There's a much smarter way. Much smarter. Do you have any idea what it is? Perhaps you're thinking that you could wait until the dollar comes roaring back against foreign currencies.

If that's what you're thinking, then I'm sorry to burst your bubble, but the dollar is fairly well priced given the sorry state of affairs in Washington. The politicians there spend over $1.80 for every dollar we send them. And if you think the Republicans' new "Contract with America" is going to make a big difference, then I've got some land in Florida that might interest you. Politics is pork. Always has been. Always will be. In a few

years' time, the voters will get fed up and throw
the current rascals out...in favor of the old free-
spending rascals. Why? Because people like pork!
JOSEPH

Which is why the dollar is going to continue
to slide. If you need additional historical proof of
this, then look at how the dollar performed over
the last decade. When the Japanese stock market
went on a tear, the dollar fell. When the Japanese
market plunged, the dollar fell. When Wall Street
collapsed in 1987, the dollar fell. When the Dow
recovered, the dollar fell. War broke out in the
Persian Gulf and the dollar fell. The Mexican peso
plunged and guess what the dollar did...

The dollar has become a
Yankee Doodle Dropout.

WILLIAM

The dollar has lost 85% of its value in our lifetimes. It has lost 15% against the world's major
currencies in this decade alone. So it's no wonder
that the dollar is no longer seen as a safe haven.
It's now viewed as an extension of our down-slid-
ing culture, a Yankee Doodle Dropout. You're left
with no choice but to take affirmative action.

JAMES

There is a simple way to shield yourself from

the continued freefall of the dollar. Indeed, you can recover 25% to 50% of the lost value with the three-phase strategy we'll discuss in these pages.

JOSEPH

I'm fond of comparing this three-phase strategy to electricity—because it's quite similar. As you know, the lowest level of electricity is single phase. Most appliances run on this. It's 120 volts with two wires—one hot, one cold. Pretty standard, low level stuff.

By analogy, most investors have single-phase portfolios. They own what they think is a "hot basket" of mutual funds, stocks, and bonds. But the bulk of their assets are "on ice" in CDs, T-bills, and money market funds.

Add it all up, and the returns are barely keeping pace with inflation. As with electricity, it's low-level stuff.

The thing is, though, you can easily upgrade that portfolio with a minimum of effort and no loss of safety. It's not a matter of upgrading to double-phase power . . . since there is no such animal.

The next level in electricity is single phase, 220 volts. Here you have three wires and two hot legs, allowing you to run bigger appliances more cost-efficiently. But it's still a low-level system. Basically, this kind of portfolio would be beefed up with high-yielding international growth stocks and maybe a rental property or a limited partnership deal.

WILLIAM

Twenty years ago, I was happy to upgrade to that level.

JOSEPH

Yes, it was a good start. But you soon learned the value of upgrading to triple-phase.

As in electricity, you get the most bang from three-phase power.

Triple-phase power is a whole new experience. You have four wires. Three are hot, one goes to ground. These are used to run big A/C units, drill presses, that kind of thing. They're extremely cost-efficient and they're also versatile. By swapping any two of the wires, you can reverse direction. That is, you can turn the motor the other way.

WILLIAM

Which is the essential point you're driving at.

JOSEPH

Absolutely. In investing, it's smart and

indeed vital to be able to change course and
realign your portfolio on a moment's notice.
You have to be ready to move from one country
to another . . . from one investment to another
. . . from one broker to another . . . without being
locked into one investment course.

The dramatic rise…and then fall…of the
global markets—especially Mexico—makes this
case very well.

And a three-phase investment strategy
ensures that you remain flexible. You will never
be locked into a loser. You will never be caught
offguard by a whipsawing market. You will be
steered safely around the rip-offs that derail the
investors who are stuck in single-phase strategies.

You will never again settle for empty platitudes such as "buy low, sell high."

You will, in short, be given all the tools you
need to seize all the wealth you desire. Let us
now continue . . . with the first step you must
take to move on up to secure ground.

Phase I

Move Onto Secure Ground

The Oxford Portfolio Top Holdings

1994		1993		1992	
Caledonia Mining	1380%	Hoffman LaRoche	104%	Hopewell Holdings	290%
Argosy Mining	170%	Hopewell Holdings	100%	Siam Cement	140%
Telebras	49%	Bank Int'l Settlem'ts	77%	Tian An	64%
Holderbank	32%	Singapore Airlines	67%	Cifra	64%
Singapore Airlines	28%	Thai Capital Fund	60%	Nikkei Put Warrants	53%
CEPA	24%	Latin Amer. Inv. Fund	56%	Tecogen	46%
Nestle	18%	Siemans	47%	Banacci	44%
Bangkok Bank	15%	Southwestern Bell	45%	New England Electric	39%
Bank Int'l Settlem'ts	12%	Royal Dutch Petrol	32%	Asia Pacific Fund	37%
Yearly Gain	192%	Yearly Gain	65.3%	Yearly Gain	86.3%

Chapter Two

A MAN'S RIGHT TO LUXURY RETIREMENT

*Why settle for a cat food retirement
when people in your same position
are upgrading to caviar?*

WILLIAM

Remember when we used to pluck out the gray hairs or suck in the belly at the first glimpse of a beautiful woman? When did things change?

When did we start thinking less about women than money? When did old age become more real than our years of youth?

JOSEPH

Don't know. I do know that I've spent a lifetime ignoring the ticking clock and even now I find it difficult to talk about the "R" word.

JAMES

Ah yes, *retirement!* It has always been such an abstraction, like a modern painting, something to "ooh" and "aah" at and then wonder what all the fuss is about.

WILLIAM

I can tell you this, I never paid any attention to the need for secure ground in retirement until a recent conversation I had with my father. He's getting on in years, having long since retired to Florida, and he finally confided his One Big Fear.

My father's One Big Fear in retirement was that he might have to ask me for money.

Dad worried that he might run through his money before he ran through his life. He had this picture of himself piling all his things into a mule cart and coming to live with me.

If Dad ever needed my help, I'd give it lickety-split. After all he's done for me, you bet I would. But it would disgrace him to have to ask. It would be an admission of failure. He'd rather have me bragging to my friends about how much money he's still making off his investments.

JOSEPH

But not too many people are bragging these days. And those who haven't yet seen the writing on the wall . . . they're in for a rude awakening.

JAMES

Which is why so many financial advisors are

issuing dire warnings and handing out worksheets to help people figure out the amount of
money they'll need to retire comfortably. But all
their drum-banging is worthless. What good is
there in trying to plan a "comfortable" retirement? A man who has worked hard all his life
and made wise decisions ought to retire in luxury. Let someone else run out of money and get
by on cat food, we want to be eating caviar! That
is the Oxford Club way!

It can be yours too . . . if you want to make it
so. There are only two things to do.

First, see if the Club can steer you safely
around today's Four Retirement Wreckers. Then
if so, tie into the one retirement plan in this
entire world *that's worth a darn*. We'll talk more
about that plan as soon as we escort you safely
past the retirement wreckers.

WILLIAM

Retirement Wrecker #1 is the most obvious—it's your pension plan. I certainly hope
that you don't expect it to pay out nearly as
much as you were once told it would.

JOSEPH

The average American expects his pension to
cover 28% of his retirement, but it's only cover-
ing 16% now. Some pension plans haven't kept

up with the cost of living. Others have been gutted by unscrupulous management. It's a crime.

Not only that, but Social Security benefits will only cover another 38% of the average retirement. This means that most people are going to have to pay about half of all their retirement bills out of their investments earnings.

Millions of Americans will run through their money before they run through life.

James

People are starting to find out that they'll have to earn $35,000 to $75,000 a year from their investments . . . in order to retire comfortably. Once they learn this shocking news, they panic and run down to their local retirement expert, usually some novice who just started shaving. That sets them up for Retirement Wrecker #2.

They get tied into a "retirement plan" that's the financial equivalent of three strikes and you're out.

Strike One: The plan is so conservative that it doesn't even keep pace with inflation and broker's fees and administration costs. They lose money by having money in the plan.

Strike Two: The plan doesn't take into account some big tax advantages that are now available. A recent survey found that 74% of CPAs didn't know all the tax breaks a retired person is entitled to. So they lose money by paying taxes they don't need to pay.

Strike three: This one is the most dangerous because it involves the law. One in four of the retirement plans that people are relying on today are technically illegal. If people don't get their money out of these plans soon, they could forfeit 35% to 50% of their retirement nest egg.

JOSEPH

The Club steers you clear of these retirement wreckers by debunking the advice being peddled by brokers and the financial media. We take these novices to task, showing you how foolish, flawed, and faulty their advice can be.

Ever made a lot of money reading the financial pages?

We have no grudge with the financial press and the big-name newsletters. I subscribe to several and I know William and James do too. But we know better than to pay too close attention to their investment advice.

We know that if a story runs in *The Wall Street Journal*, for example, it means that millions of people are reading it, thousands saw it pre-publication, and a few hundred acted on it before the reporter ever got the details.

That makes it as stale as last month's bread.

The trick is to invest the way those few hundred did. You need to have someone letting you in on the investment secrets while they are still secrets. That's where the Club comes in. Our international network of insiders and experts gets the information long before it ever goes public.

I'm reminded of how the Club networking concept pays off. A few months ago, one of our Members who happens to be a diamond expert got wind of an exciting strike in the Northwest Territories. He phoned in to our U.S. offices and suggested that we take a closer look before the whole world learned about it.

We dispatched our Financial Director to snoop around and sure enough, gigantic profits were in the offing. Soon after, the entire Membership was alerted. Those who acted right away saw the stock of this Canadian mining company zoom up from $.77 to $11.40 (Canadian) in our first year!

That's a mouth-watering, millionaire-making 1,380% profit and all because of our networking system. (You'll read more about this diamond bonanza on page 57.)

Members helping Members to get the profits first.

We scored those 1,000-to-1 returns because we knew how to make good advance use of superior knowledge. We knew better than to wait around until it ran in the financial media.

JAMES

I've found that it takes new Members only a few months "on the inside" before they fully understand that most of what passes for *news* is actually *olds*.

But this next matter . . . Retirement Wrecker #3 . . . is a tougher nut to crack. It involves interest rates, and it cuts deep for most of us. That's because most of us have planned out our retirements on the assumption of high interest rates.

JOSEPH

For years, it seemed to make sense. High interest rates made bonds an easy play. Bonds were turning in 15% to 20% yields like clockwork, and would continue to, or so it appeared—once again reminding us that nothing lasts forever. Today, those same bonds are yielding a paltry 3% to 5% if you're lucky.

But a lot of people are still holding onto those bonds because they're stuck in an inflationary mindset. They figure that it's just a matter of time before the low rates pass and they start making the easy money again. But they're figuring wrong.

I cannot emphasize enough that no matter

what you do—whether you choose to join the Club or not—do not fool around in the bond market for the next several years. You can't win.

WILLIAM

This talk about interest rates leads us naturally to Retirement Wrecker #4—a little thing called inflation.

Having a little inflation is like being a little pregnant.

JAMES

Inflation has supposedly been tamed, and nobody worries too much about it anymore, but that only makes it worse. Even a low 5% inflation rate means that the luxury $100,000 a year retirement of today will, by 2012, cost well in excess of $250,000!

Let's say that you're retiring today at the ripe old age of 65 and that you will live to be 100. It's happening more and more, you know! Just to maintain your lifestyle you will need a mind-boggling $8.75 million.

That's a whole lot more than most of us have stashed away. And that, ultimately, is why most retirement plans are worthless. As I said earlier, there is only one retirement plan worth a darn.

This plan wouldn't work if the whole world found out about it.

This plan addresses all 4 retirement wreckers. It does not involve any demeaning worksheets that calculate the exact amount you need to make it to your 80th, 90th, or 100th birthday. None of that. This plan is as foolproof as it is vital to your future.

This plan is, simply, to earn more from your investments than you could ever hope to spend in three lifetimes!

Make more money than you could spend in 3 lifetimes!

How can you make so much? All the tools and knowledge you need are waiting for you in the Oxford Club. The first of these tools may be the most exciting and profitable—it will certainly give you a keen advantage in the buying and selling of investments. It is the subject of the next session.

The Oxford Portfolio Top Holdings

1994	1993	1992	
Caledonia Mining 1380%	Hoffman LaRoche 104%	Hopewell Holdings	290%
Argosy Mining 170%	Hopewell Holdings 100%	Siam Cement	140%
Telebras 49%	Bank Int'l Settlem'ts 77%	Tian An	64%
Holderbank	Singapore Airlines 67%	Cifra	64%
Sin…	… 6?%	Nikkei Put Warrants	53%
CH…		Tecogen	46%
Nes…		Banacci	44%
Ba…		New England Electric	39%
Bank Int'l settlem'ts 12%	Royal Dutch Petrol 52%	Asia Pacific Fund	37%
Yearly Gain 192%	Yearly Gain 65.3%	Yearly Gain	86.3%

> **1993 HOFFMAN LaROCHE** — Many of our star performers are common household names— making it easy to invest with confidence.

Chapter Three

A MAN'S RIGHT TO PERFECT KNOWLEDGE

New computer programs allow scientists to select winning investments with 80% accuracy. Ever done that well?

JAMES

In our last session, I told you about a tool that will give you an advantage in the buying and selling of investments. It is a tool that Joseph has been developing for many years. A tool that allows us to analyze the financial world, to take it apart and see how it works and then put it back together in a way that helps our Members make money. Lots of it. Joseph?

JOSEPH

A little history would be in order first. Back when I was a kid, I loved to take things apart. That's pretty typical for boys, I know. But I would put them back together, and make them better, at least most of the time. My mother wasn't always so thrilled about it. Like the time in '41 when I made a little gas-powered cart out of an old tiller we had. I broke my collarbone and almost tore down the toolshed when it went haywire. Gas rationing and my mother put an end to my carting days for a while.

But that love of tinkering, taking things apart, analyzing them, has stuck with me all my life. That's why I became a physics professor and why I wanted to understand the natural order of things, the predictability of things. About this time, I also got interested in investing. It wasn't too long before I saw an interesting connection between the two.

Foretell the future and the money will follow.

One of my heroes has always been Andy Capp, that shaggy little Englishman in comics. There's a strip where Andy gets asked by the bar-keep which he'd choose—money, power, happiness, or seeing the future? Well, Andy chooses "seeing the future." He figures that the power of foresight will make him money; money will bring him power, and power will bring him happiness.

Therein lay the connection I referred to.

While I was doing my post-graduate work, I began studying the writings of Dr. Theodore Modis and Cesare Marchetti of the International Institute of Advanced Systems Analysis, in Austria. They have made breakthroughs in the study of natural phenomena known as *invariants*. It sounds like heady stuff, I know, but you can follow it easily.

A good example of an invariant is the fact that mammals all die at the same age. Does that sound wrong to you? Not when you think about life in terms of heartbeats. All mammals have about a billion heartbeats in them. Mice only live three years, but their little hearts pound away a billion times. Elephants live for 50 years, but their hearts thump slowly. The human heart is good for about a billion, too, beaten out over 80 or 90 years.

WILLIAM

This is all fascinating stuff, Joseph. But what's the connection between these invariants and making money hand over fist?

JOSEPH

They are inseparable! Physicists have applied these natural laws to the commercial world, to product life-cycles, to corporate earnings. They have found that the natural laws, if applied correctly, can make investment forecasts more reliable.

**These natural laws make
investment forecasts
more reliable.**

WILLIAM

The forecasts would have to be "more reliable" by a factor of ten. Most economists are no better than weathermen at making accurate predictions.

JOSEPH

Because economists and weathermen are of the same beast. They call what they do a science . . . but it's more like black magic. They make models. They devise fancy equations. But they are completely dependant on the variables they plug into the computer. Plug in the wrong variables, and the models crash.

Plus, they are trying to predict short-term, which is a thankless business. Physicists go about it differently. We don't allow ourselves to get caught up in the short-term and 1,001 variables. We look at whole systems over time.

We believe that the elements in a system will act in a certain invariant way, bringing out the system's *fingerprint*—its pattern of up's and down's as well as the fundamental laws that govern its past, present, and future. These fingerprints can be mapped with something known as an *S-curve*.

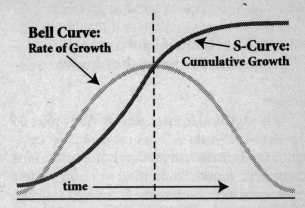

Unlike its cousin, the bell-curve, the S-curve can be of immense value in predicting investment life cycles.

You are familiar with the standard bell curve. It depicts probabilities and distributions of events—which is all fine and good. But as investors, we want to know how fast our investments will grow and when they will stop growing. The S-curve gives us this valuable information.

JAMES

Let me interrupt, Joseph. If I had never heard of your S-curves, and didn't know a thing about their predictive power, I would wonder why Wall Street doesn't know about them.

The financial gurus aren't telling you what they know.

JOSEPH

The top money managers on Wall Street do know about S-curves. They use neural net computers to generate curves that would make Jane Mansfield proud. But most investors know nothing of them because the gurus aren't talking. They want to keep their comfortable positions on top of the financial heap.

WILLIAM

Can you compute an S-curve on any kind of investment?

JOSEPH

You can compute them on any *thing*. On the number of sea voyages west before Columbus embarked. On the number of years it will take before the Cubs win the World Series. And yes, on the growth of investments.

For instance, one of my hobbies is mountain climbing. So for the fun of it, I computed the number of people that can be expected to climb Mt. Whitney in coming years.

To do it, I plugged all the data available on

past expeditions into my computer program. I let the computer run all weekend. I came in on Monday to find that when my information input was 90% to 95% correct, then the prediction going out was at least 80% correct.

I have only begun to tell you all I know about S-curves and the natural laws. But it all boils down to this: When I know at least half of the history of something, I can tell you what the other half will be.

Make money on 8 out of 10 investments you buy.

JAMES

Forecast an industry for us, Joseph. Using your S-curves, tell us what the outlook is for the U.S. auto industry.

JOSEPH

Auto industry, eh? We know they're hurting. Sure, Detroit has won back some of the market share they've lost to imports, but the fix is in. To show you how and why, let's do an S-curve on transportation in America. Looking back over time, we see a very orderly evolution.

Every 50 to 60 years, transportation history has turned topsy-turvy and everything old has become suddenly new. First, it was the canals and inland waterways that opened up millions of acres of fertile grains to the marketplace. Then the railways that connected the coasts. Then the interstate highway system that opened cities everywhere. Most recently, it has been the airways that have altered the way we live.

The Rise of Primary Transportation Modes

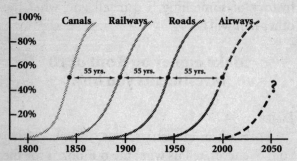

The big investment profits are made when the S-curves tilt up.

But the important thing for the investor to grasp is the "time frames." If you chart these big changes, you will see that they've come along every 50 to 60 years. Once the cycle has been completed, and a new one has begun, most of the big excitement and profit-making from the old cycle has disappeared.

The S-curve for autos was growing at its

fastest pace in 1965, not coincidentally paralleling the success of the Mustang. But now, the U.S. car makers have seen their best days. The market is 90% saturated. The industry will become a supplier of replacement cars and parts only. No great leaps in production.

It's the same with highway construction. The government will continue to maintain the roads we've got, but there won't be any infrastructure creation of note. Not in this country, anyway.

WILLIAM

So anything having to do with the auto will be a bad investment?

JOSEPH

There will be pockets of opportunity. But the uptilting growth curve in U.S. autos is behind us. In fact, we have already seen most of the big growth in the airline industry, too.

A new S-curve points the way to tomorrow's profits.

WILLIAM

So what is the next big transportation trend?

JOSEPH

Around the world, people will be looking to

low-polluting, high-capacity transport. Maglevs, or magnetic levitation trains, will come into wide use around the year 2000. Then that trend will run its 50 to 60 year course.

More important to us now is an allied trend—the transporting of information electronically. What's being called the "information superhighway" will change our lives in ways we can't begin to envision. The Oxford Club is already researching the best investments for you to make…at the proper time in this S-curve…to bring home truly stellar returns in the coming years.

WILLIAM

Isn't it about time we talk about some of those "well-placed investments" and give some specifics? Names and numbers?

JAMES

Yes, it is. We've now outlined the tools we use to move our Members' finances onto secure ground. It's time to move onto the second phase of our power strategy.

Phase II
Lead
To Your
Strength

The Oxford Portfolio Top Holdings

1994		1993		1992	
Caledonia Mining	1380%	Hoffman LaRoche	104%	Hopewell Holdings	290%
Argosy Mining	179%	In...		Siam Cement	140%
Telebras	49%	Ba...		Tian An	64%
Holderbank	32%	Si...		Cifra	64%
Singapore Airlines	28%	Th...		Nikkei Put Warrants	53%
CEPA	24%	La...		Tecogen	46%
Nestle	18%	Si...		**Banacci**	**44%**
Bangkok Bank	15%	So...		New England Electric	39%
Bank Int'l Settlem'ts	12%	Roy...		Asia Pacific Fund	37%
Yearly Gain	192%	Yearly Gain	65.3%	Yearly Gain	86.3%

> **1992 BANACCI** — Banacci was an early Oxford Club foray into Mexico's burgeoning economy—bringing us 44% profits.

Chapter Four

A MAN'S RIGHT TO GRAND PROFITS

*Invest in today's blue chips for good profits;
invest in the breakthrough blue chips of
tomorrow for grand profits.*

WILLIAM

Here's a name for you—Thaddeus Mazujes-ki. Ring any bells? You might know him by his professional name—Teddy Majestic. One of the best professional poker players of all time. Teddy's semi-retired now. He splits his time between his custom-designed, ten-room Swiss chalet in the Rockies . . . and traveling the country teaching people to not be afraid of success, to dare to be rich.

The other day, Teddy was telling Members why he finally decided to quit the professional circuit. Teddy loves poker. He'll play with any-one, but not for big stakes. He's got a rule about that. He won't play a big stakes game until he's gotten to know you.

As for why he quit, well, a few years ago, one of Teddy's backers approached him with an offer. There was a Brazilian businessman who wanted to play him. For big money.

Teddy refused the challenge at first. His backer kept pressing, however, and then pleading. Finally Teddy gave in. The backer was a friend, after all. The game was set up in a plush hotel in Rio.

Teddy did pretty well for the first three hours. Red chips piled up and then the blue. Then boom! The businessman started playing wildly and threw Teddy's game off kilter. By the end of the evening, the Brazilian had won the pot.

Teddy was disgusted that he had been wheedled into breaking one of his first rules of the game. It's a rule that he says applies to winning at poker and winning at investing. For that matter, it's a good rule of life.

It's a simple rule, but one we often forget:

You want to win? Know the players in the game!

If you intend to win the game, especially when the stakes matter, you've got to know the players. You got to know who's holding the cards, and how they intend to play them. That's how you win and then keep on winning.

JOSEPH

The Oxford Club offers men an invitation to

the Big Game. We know the world's markets—
we've been playing them for decades. We have
the added advantage of the S-curves—predictive
tools that give you the edge you need to compete.
Now, let's start stacking some of those blue chips
in your corner.

JAMES

Joseph is setting us up to hear about the best
blue-chip investments on the seven continents
today. I can tell you that the three of us are looking forward to this next session as much as I trust
you are. We are about to receive our latest insider briefing from the Club's research director.
He's scheduled to unveil his picks for the 1994-95
investment period.

>   *James clicks a remote control. From
>   the ornate ceiling of the old manor, a large
>   video screen lowers. A digital display indi-
>   cates 1140 hours in Zurich. A man on
>   the screen waves to his three friends.*

It's my pleasure to introduce Christopher
Weber, the Research Director and Financial Editor of the Oxford Club.

Of Austrian descent, Christopher is a man
with singular financial vision. At an early age, he
studied with the masters of the acclaimed Austri-

an School of Economics where he refined and sharpened his libertarian principles.

Stricken with a wanderlust, Christopher then traveled to nearly every capitalist country. Along the way, he developed a financial intelligence network that served him well as an investment advisor.

His first clients, back in the '70s, were European banks that sought to develop financial footholds in the coming European market. Christopher made it happen, and along the way, made quite a name for himself.

A man of unbounded energy, Christopher has written seven books on investing, including the long-time international bestseller, *The Austrian Advantage*.

It was while he was working on his latest book, *Getting Rich Outside the Dollar*, that Christopher's path collided with ours. Having made a second home in the United States, he was studying the peculiar way that Americans approach investing.

He was aware that very few Americans ever invest overseas. But in his research, he came across a group of Americans who were quite comfortable investing, as they put it, "wherever in the world the getting was good." He was fascinated by these investors and wanted to learn as much as he could about them.

Who were these Americans?

Why were these people different? How could they be so comfortable in their dealings? What made it possible for them to move between the New York, London, and Hong Kong markets with the same acrobatic ease that wealthy Europeans had long practiced? These were the questions Christopher sought answers to.

Soon, he found that it had to do with the nature of the club they belonged to. Called the Oxford, the Club brought the best of old world academia to the rough-and-tumble of modern American investing. It discriminated against no one, though it was extraordinarily picky in who it would favor for Membership.

Christopher made a point of attending a chapter meeting in Florida where he met Club Director Julia Guth.

He began feeding investment recommendations to the Club, and his recommendations proved both insightful and profitable. The rest, as they say, is history.

Now I give you Christopher.

CHRISTOPHER

Hello James, William, Joseph. And greetings to our prospective Member. I bring a very short list of six stocks to this briefing. As you know, I

would rather give you just a few solid gems than a
big plateful of dust.

JOSEPH

I should point out that this is the approach
Christopher takes in the Club's monthly communiques. He focuses in on one or two issues,
and develops them fully, so that you are never left
wanting or wondering. It's an approach that I
know you'll value.

CHRISTOPHER

Thank you, Joseph. Let me say right up front
that I'm very encouraged by the stock picks I
bring today. Every one is a winner. Every one
has the potential to turn $1,000 into $5,000…or
$10,000 into $100,000…before the decade's end.
Each one of them is a breakthrough blue chip of
tomorrow.

The way to capture high returns
while dodging high risks.

First, some background. These stocks are
ideal for people who want to shoot for the big
returns but can't handle the big risks of start-ups,
options, commodities and the like.

I've called these "breakthrough" blue chips
because they are vital and alive and poised to

capitalize on the hottest future trends.

These stocks are *not*, in analysts' parlance, "generals fighting the last war." If you're familiar with this military reference, you know it relates to commanders in the field who are always attempting to redo what worked in the last campaign. Unfortunately, as we recently saw in Mexico, it seldom works.

If you are following one of the popular investment advisors, chances are you're getting stuck in rigid, inflexible thinking.

These advisors think they're doing you a favor by surveying who made most money last year, or what strategies worked in the last market cycle, then repeating the formula. Only, nine times in ten, the situation has changed and the old winners are the new losers.

To succeed in investing, you have to act, not react. If you want to win in the future, whether at war or investing, you have to look into the future. And, you have to do your homework.

WILLIAM

Or have the Oxford Club do it for you. Christopher, are these six companies all global players?

CHRISTOPHER

Yes, which is another reason I'm so excited. Each one is capitalizing on the global rush to capitalism. They trade on exchanges from Canada to Hong Kong, but you can buy them just like you do U.S. stocks on U.S. exchanges.

To give you an idea how we expect these picks to perform, let's review the actual performance of our complete list of Top 10 holdings for 1994:

1)	**Caledonia Mining**	1380%
2)	**Argosy Mining**	170%
3)	**Telebras**	49%
4)	**Holderbank**	32%
5)	**Singapore Airlines**	28%
6)	**CEPA**	24%
7)	**Nestle**	18%
8)	**Bangkok Bank**	15%
9)	**Bank for Int'l Settlements**	12%
10)	**Royal Dutch Shell**	11%

Add up the numbers, and you'll see that the Club's top 10 picks netted Members average profits of 180% and let me tell you this—NO OTHER NEWSLETTER EVEN CAME CLOSE.

Most others had losing years. The S&P was 3% in the tank. But we averaged 180% over a complete portfolio of 10 stocks. Plus, we've done just about as well in the last four years. So yes, I'm expecting the same high returns over the next 24-36 months from the breakthrough blue chips I'm now recommending. Each of these stocks has a steady track record, and each is selling for $10 or less a share so you can buy in easily.

Best of all, these stocks are not particularly well known to the American investment community.

WILLIAM

How can a "breakthrough" stock not be discovered in today's instant communications world?

CHRISTOPHER

You've heard of pack journalism? Well, there's also a phenomenon called "pack stock coverage." At least 90% of the Wall Street regulars all read the same newspapers, hear the same gossip, and follow the same analysis. And when you're following a herd of bulls, guess what you're stepping in?

Don't get me wrong, I listen to the crowd. But I prefer to strike out on my own, visiting companies unannounced, sizing them in the ruff, and only then returning to my office to crunch the numbers.

JOSEPH

What numbers do you look at?

Christopher

P/E ratios, earnings projections, profit margins, return-on-stockholders equity, and a dozen others. In this regard, I'm no better than any other analyst.

I think what makes my picks superior is the field research I do. When I'm out traveling, I make it a point to meet with the right people at the right places. In men's clubs, along private beaches, on cruises with European banking friends, that's how I get the extra edge. Often it will be a few choice words, spoken in a code known only to the old pros, that will launch me on a new hunt for virgin opportunities.

Tell us what's in your private trove!

These six stock picks may be the finest group I've ever assembled. The first and most delightfully boring of the six is one the Membership already knows. I recommended it initially in January 1994, and it's still a solid buy.

It's Holderbank, and it appreciated 32% last year even as the rest of the market was taking a nosedive.

Holderbank sounds like a bank, but it's actually the world's largest cement producer. Nothing in this whole wide world seems as boring as cement. Nothing! And that's why it's so good.

You see, if you follow stocks for a living—believe me, you don't want to be caught dead following the most boring industry in the world. But to me, cement is gray gold, and do you know why?

What's the biggest news from Kuala Lumpur to Rio?

People are building! They're doing what America did in the '60s and '70s and '80s. Roads, apartment complexes, shopping malls, airports. Using billions of metric tons of cement every month. Cement that someone has to supply. Cement that can bring you real, hard profits.

The great thing is, much of the world's cement is made by one company, none other than Holderbank. This gray Goliath operates 30 wholly-owned subsidiaries in places around the globe where wages are low but building is brisk. It controls Cerro Blanco—Chile's best, and Apasco—Mexico's best.

Despite all this, Holderbank's price/earnings ratio is only half as pricey as the average U.S. stock. Bottom line—Holderbank is a smart move for 10% of your investment capital.

This is a Swiss company but it can be purchased with relative ease and even at a discount from the right stateside brokers. I give you all the 'how to' and 'why for' details in a special follow-up briefing I've written…titled *The Breakthrough Blue Chips of Tomorrow.*

JOSEPH

Your follow-up briefing won't just provide raw data, will it?

No raw information, only actionable knowledge.

CHRISTOPHER

I see no value in giving raw information that "informs" and nothing more. You need hard knowledge so that you "know" what's going on and can make intelligent decisions.

You need hard knowledge to make the right stock purchase with a reputable broker who knows international markets.

You need hard knowledge to follow your stock with an eagle eye . . . and ultimately sell for a grand profit. My follow-up briefing will accomplish just that.

It will also steer you straight on my next favorite—the airline that you fellows flew into Hong Kong on one of your last profit-seeking junkets. This airline has been doing something that is unique in all the industry—*they've been making money!* While the U.S. airlines have been losing billions, this airline made $600 million in pure profit last year alone.

I'm speaking about none other than Singapore Airlines—the one with the beautiful women in their ads and more to the point, the one that has been posting the highest profits in the industry for the last three years running.

Soon to join the world's 100 premier blue chips.

Singapore Airlines' balance sheet is solid. They have $1.8 billion in cold cash . . . in the bank . . . right now. They have a dividend that's steadily increasing and a stock price that's only 12 times earnings. In ten years, this airline will not only be the most profitable one in the world, it may well be the largest.

WILLIAM
That's a bold projection.

JOSEPH
Not really. As we discussed earlier, I ran an S-curve on the U.S. airline industry and found them 60% through their quantum growth period. But the international airlines are newer, and people the world over are taking to the air the way Americans did in the '60s and '70s. Consequent-

ly, the international airlines are only now entering the quantum growth aspect of their S-curve.

CHRISTOPHER

And of all the international carriers, Singapore Airlines is the sweetest success story. Their future prospects are even rosier because they have an excellent route system, a young fleet of planes, they're cornering the home turf, and they're creating strategic alliances with other regional carriers to propel them to the top.

Their stock moved up a handsome 28% last year, and I expect a continued upward lift for years to come. Ten years from now this airline may well rank among the world's top 100 blue chips.

As upbeat as I am about this airline, I'm even more excited about our next investment. This one has already turned every $10 we've invested into $1,380! It's one of the Club's all-time greatest picks.

After a stock soars 1,380%, can it soar another 1,380?

In the last few weeks, I've been asked by dozens of Members what to do now with our super-successful mining speculation, Caledonia Mining Company. For those new to this stock, let me tell you an incredible story.

Caledonia Mining is not one of those flash-in-the-pan outfits. The company's managers have been in the diamond mining business for thirty years. They own millions of acres of diamond claims around the world. On top of that, they own producing gold, stone, and marble mines throughout Europe. Now they're sitting on what could be the discovery of the century. They may have tapped into the richest diamond lode in modern history. It could become a modern-day Golconda.

But, even if the discovery never pans out, this classy mining company can still be counted on to churn out 10% to 20% profits throughout the decade. So you really can't lose by taking a flyer on this stock.

Their amazing story began when another exploration company, Dia Met Minerals, discovered a horde of diamonds in kimberlite pipes near Lac de Gras in the Northwest Territories. Right away, of course, Dia Met's stock shot through the ceiling and investors raked in a fortune. It's too late to buy Dia Met now, but an even better opportunity has arisen in Caledonia Mining.

Could this discovery be the next Golconda?

With their experience working for DeBeers

in South Africa, they know what it means when
diamonds are found in the magnesium-rich
kimberlite pipes.

For every carat that is found in the pipes,
they've learned that 30 carats have eroded and
been carried along the river beds out to sea. For
this reason, these shrewd miners moved quickly
to stake their claim to over half a million acres
along the five rivers that drain Lac de Gras to the
gulf, as well as much of the coast and offshore
islands fed by the rivers.

WILLIAM

When will we know if they've hit the jackpot?

CHRISTOPHER

It's still early in the game. But there has been
good news already. Caledonia has been finding
"indicator minerals" which means that diamonds couldn't be far behind.

If diamonds are found, the stock will shoot up again.

If diamonds are found, Caledonia's stock
could easily shoot up another 1,380% and for
one very special reason.

DeBeers. That's right, the South African
DeBeers organization will pay any price to keep

their iron-fisted control over world diamond production. They will move immediately to snap up Caledonia, and if you own shares in it, you will see your foresight amply rewarded.

OTC Price Graph for Caledonia Mining

(in Canadian dollars)

1/7/94   1/13/95

The stock has shot up from C$.77 to C$11.40 in the twelve months that the Oxford Club has been recommending it. I would advise Members to keep an eye on it, wait for weakness in the markets, then try to pick it up under $7 if possible.

Purchase at least 100 shares for starters. It's possible that no diamonds will be found, in which case you will own a solid company that's posting 15% to 20% profits a year. But if diamonds are found ...

Then it's Katy bar the door and Molly tap the keg—because a $1,000 investment could easily become $140,000 or even better! It has already happened to some of our Members. It could happen to you.

To learn everything you need to know about

Caledonia Mining as well as my other top picks for 1995 and 1996, get your hands on my follow-up briefing, *The Breakthrough Blue Chips of Tomorrow*. I can personally guarantee that this briefing will put you on solid financial ground.

On that note, gentlemen, I'll sign off.

JAMES

Thank you, Christopher. We look forward to receiving a copy of the follow-up briefing and passing it along to the Membership.

James clicks the remote, and the video screen lifts into the ceiling and disappears.

WILLIAM

After everything that Christopher has told us about Caledonia, perhaps we should talk about the best way to buy Canadian stocks.

JAMES

That subject will be covered in the third phase of our power strategy. Right now, we have other money-making ideas to discuss.

Chapter Five

A MAN'S RIGHT TO REAL ESTATE

Looking to ride the new wave in real estate?
Or move to tomorrow's retirement haven?
Look no further.

JAMES

Of all our rights, none is more sacrosanct than the right to hold private property. Our Founding Fathers held *Life, Liberty,* and *Property* in the highest regard.

It was only after bitter debate that they changed Thomas Jefferson's wording in the Declaration of Independence to *Life, Liberty,* and the *Pursuit of Happiness.*

We at the Oxford Club prefer Jefferson's earlier version, but who are we to quibble?

JOSEPH

Most men come to our Club with a substantial portfolio. Their net worth is between $500,000 and $1.5 million. They own some real estate and may be looking to purchase another property either in the States or overseas. For this reason, the Club keeps an active file on the choicest properties and white-collar addresses of tomorrow.

Capitalize on the growing white-collar migration.

We make this information available to Members in our regular briefings, special reports and "hands-on" field expeditions. In addition, you can always call your Member Services Liaison and request information on a subject of interest to you.

WILLIAM

For real estate investors, it is an exciting time. After several years of sitting in the doldrums, we are now on the cusp of an explosive real estate market. Property prices are rebounding in key buying areas. There couldn't be a better time to invest. Not only that, but America is undergoing a massive migration unlike anything in its history. This is a "white-collar" migration and the reasons for it are well known.

The suburbs have become pricey, congested, polluted, unsafe and largely unlivable. Millions of people are getting fed up and moving to fairer climates, where the living is easy and property is still affordable. Club Members who make savvy real estate buys at the current market lows… can expect values to double by the turn of the century.

JAMES

Most people will miss or dismiss this white-collar migration. They will look to buy in the wrong places. They will use old-fashioned yard-sticks. They will rely on the advice of real estate salesmen and money magazines. And that's just fine with us. Because here at the Oxford Club, we know where tomorrow's hottest addresses will be.

We know how computers, faxes, modems and teleconferencing are reorganizing the nation. We have been using the tools of the information superhighway for nearly a decade now.

Bottom line—we've uncovered the choicest unspoiled havens to invest in or move to. We've found prosperous little nooks and crannies along the road less traveled, and we've taken good notes. Our staffs in Zurich, London, Washington, and Baltimore have compiled all of our findings into a massive database that is available to the Membership.

If you are looking for property that can be counted on to double in desirability and thus profitability, then you owe it to yourself to learn more about the Oxford Club database.

You'll discover magical counties with names like Shelby, Alabama . . . Douglas, Colorado . . . Fayette, Georgia . . . Fort Bend, Texas. These are fast-growing pockets of wealth. They will be enjoying 20% annual growth in the '90s, and real estate investment doesn't get any better.

JOSEPH

Some people are under the impression that prices in the "plum areas" have been driven up by the last few years of growth.

WILLIAM

That's what they told Bob Hope and Bing Crosby before they recorded *Make The San Fernando Valley My Home,* and then quickly bought up every open parcel in the valley. Our country is still growing, not shrinking. People are migrating to places where their hard-earned dollars can still buy a slice of the American dream.

JAMES

Yes they are. Although, in recent years, our Members have been asking less and less about "American" dream havens and more and more about "overseas" havens. Many people who have worked hard all their lives and who are now looking for a little slice of retirement heaven can't find it in the States.

These are people who are proud to be Americans, but they have begun looking at the offshore option. Perhaps you feel the same way . . .

and are interested in learning more about the living, investment, and retirement opportunities overseas.

If so, then you will be excited to learn more about the Club's profit-seeking junkets.

These profit-seeking junkets will have your eyes popping.

Several times a year, we shove off in search of adventure, exhilaration, and money-making opportunities. Our purpose is a perfectly delightful one—to go to the far ends of the earth if that's what it takes to insure a man's right to real estate (and other facets of wealth).

JOSEPH

In the last decade, Members have taken expeditions to dozens of countries, from China to Chile. We've toured prime real estate, met with local bankers to hammer out financing packages, and locked up lucrative business deals with local entrepreneurs.

As a result of these high-level meetings, a number of Members have developed their own thriving businesses and retirement getaways in overseas garden paradises.

I recently participated in an expedition to the Central American country of Belize. And I can tell you this, we all returned home buzzing. We found Belize to be an international man's paradise.

Nestled between Mexico and Guatemala, Belize offers a wide range of climates and opportunities. There are deserted white-sand beaches, clear-flowing waterfalls amid ancient Mayan ruins, fishing off the world's longest living barrier reef, bird watching in a rain forest that also supplies an abundant harvest of natural healing plants, and that's only the start.

Amidst all this wonder is the greatest wonder of all: There are still tremendous buys to be had in real estate.

I was so impressed with the values . . . I purchased some land on the fragrant shores of Ambergris Caye. I was able to buy virgin property that I expect to double or even triple in value in the next five to ten years.

Ambergris is only one of the many gorgeous properties still available. If you are interested in an overseas haven or a second home, look into the Club's files on Belize.

The most exquisite retirement haven on God's fertile earth.

The wonderful lifestyle of Belize is only the start.

Belize is safe, Democratic, and English is the national language. The country boasts a cost-of-living that's a dream come true, taxes so low that it's almost sinful, and their quality of health care will set your mind at ease at once.

It should come as no surprise, then, that a large American expatriate community is forming. Belize may well become the vacation and retirement destination of choice in the next few years.

If you would like additional information on Belize or another overseas haven, simply contact your *Member Services Liaison* and ask for a full briefing.

A Quick Review

We are two-thirds through our power strategy. In Phase One, we showed you how we can move you onto solid financial footing—by boosting your buying power, steering you clear of retirement wreckers, and perfecting your knowledge of international markets and tomorrow's trends.

Then in Phase Two, we showed you how to make the most of your portfolio—capitalizing on breakthrough blue chips and real estate bargains for handsome 40% to 125% and even 1,380% annual profits.

Now it's time for the third phase of the Oxford Club power strategy. Get ready to learn about the unlimited financial resources that the Club makes available to members.

Phase III
Never Ever Accept Losses

The Oxford Portfolio Top Holdings

1994		1993		1992	
Caledonia Mining	1380%	Hoffman LaRoche	184%	Hopewell Holdings	29(0)%
Argosy Mining	170%	Hopewell Holdings	100%		
Telebras	49%	Bank Int'l Settlem'ts	77%		
Holderbank	32%	Singapore Airlines	67%		
Singapore Airlines	28%	Thai Capital Fund	68%		
CEPA	24%	Latin Amer. Inv. Fund	5_%		
Nestle	18%	Siemans	37%		
Bangkok Bank	15%	Southwestern Bell	45%	New England Electric	39%
Bank Int'l Settlem'ts	12%	Royal Dutch Petrol	32%	Asia Pacific Fund	37%
Yearly Gain	192%	Yearly Gain	65.3%	Yearly Gain	86.3%

> **1993 Southwestern Bell** — Not all our picks are overseas. We always hold a few domestic champs—like this easy 45% gainer.

Chapter Six

A MAN'S RIGHT TO TAX-FREE LIVING

It's well known that "the rich" pay less than their fair share of taxes. It's less well known how they do it.

JOSEPH

Do you know why they call the tax form a 1040? Because 1040 was the year Lady Godiva was born. Wondering about the connection? Well, Lady Godiva was the first to lose her shirt over taxes!

WILLIAM

Taxes. Say the word and either eyes glaze over, or stomachs knot up. Most of us would love to chop a few thousand dollars off our tax bill, but not if it means hours of tedious calculations. And not if it means jumping through hoops. We hate hoops.

We'd sooner take a loss than risk a long, never-ending audit with IRS agents snooping about. When it comes to taking risks with taxes, a lot of us turn into perfect cowards.

JAMES

Which is why the Club goes to such lengths to help our Members live as tax-free as is technically and legally possible. Cutting taxes and the nervousness they cause is an essential part of the third phase of the Club power strategy. This idea behind this third phase was perhaps best articulated by Sir Winston Churchill. To misquote him slightly . . .

Never give in. Never give in. Never, never, never. Not to the needling lawyers. Not to the hoards of faceless bureaucrats and bleeding hearts. Not to the punks and the snoops who've got their eyes on your hard-earned wealth.

WILLIAM

In short, never ever accept losses. That applies first and foremost to taxes.

Go from "whining" to "winning" with taxes

JOSEPH

I'm a guy who loves numbers and equations, but I no longer enjoy working on my taxes because there's no longer any rhyme or reason to the tax code. Contradictions abound. You can be nailed even if you've done nothing wrong. One little slip can trigger an audit that can turn your life upside down for years. It can be abject hell.

WILLIAM

I know, I was audited once, over twenty years ago. That's the main reason we began this Club — to insure that I and people I cared about would never again be subjected to the harassment my wife and my children and I endured … month after month . . . for two years.

When we met so many years ago, we made a decision to attract the finest tax attorneys that money could buy to the Club.

JOSEPH

I remember asking you how we could afford tax pros who would be charging the equivalent of $300 an hour in today's economy.

WILLIAM

And I told you they would be eager to join … so that they too could take advantage of the *Oxford Club Connection* . . . the idea of everyone bringing his bit of genius to the network.

Tax Specialists showing us how to move our 1040 from the IRS's in-box to the out-box without ever raising an electronic eyebrow.

Banking Specialists taking us on actual tours of their overseas banks and helping us set up confidential accounts.

Investment Specialists roaming the world in search of revolutionary new technologies, upstart companies, the best tax-deferred investments, new market leaders, and tomorrow's trends.

This is the *Oxford Club Connection*—good profits in the company of good men, a buddy system for grown men. The perfect way— indeed the only real way that most men can insure their right to wealth.

Take advantage of the finest tax lawyers in the land.

JOSEPH

This "connection" has assured our rights, as we can all attest. Over the years, we've used the Oxford Club's tax specialists to shield ourselves from all manner of attack. There must be at least two dozen tax attorneys in the Club today. And their expertise is made available to you, as a Member, with our compliments.

JAMES

You will receive regular briefings from our specialists, and you will be invited to meet with them personally at special retreats and in *Oxford Club Chapter Meetings* in your area. Probably the first thing that'll surprise you about these briefings is the level of candor and clarity.

Our specialists aren't out to win any IRS beauty pageants or do-gooding merit badges. They're mercenaries. They're trained to ease you through the system without mishap. Whether you own a couple of complex partnerships and overseas holdings, or are simply filing the 1040EZ this year, the Oxford Club tax attorneys will go to work for you.

Our tax pros will explain to you the secrets that the rich and well-connected use to move their 1040 from the in-box to the out-box . . . without ever raising an electronic eyebrow.

Right now, to get you started, let's review a few of the *Tax-Free Living Strategies*.

The secret of the 'easy-in easy-out' tax strategy.

JOSEPH

Tax-Free Living Strategy #1 is to make it look like a pro did your return. When your 1040 is crisp, clearly organized, and filled out in the precise manner that the IRS code book dictates, your return is much more likely to sail through the system untouched.

This is because the IRS knows that a professionally prepared return will be difficult to audit and expensive to pursue. Not worth the time.

The dirty little secret of the IRS is that returns which are easy to audit get audited most often. It's true! The IRS is one of the most understaffed, shorthanded agencies of government. They always take the path of least resistance. So by doing the little things that make your return look like a veteran CPA prepared it, you build a safety net around yourself.

WILLIAM

The one purpose of each of these tax strategies is to insure that you cut your taxes to the barest minimum while sending a loud and clear message to the IRS:

"Hands off, pals!"

JOSEPH

Another way to send this message is to know which deductions to take and which not to take. There's a science to this, and it's *Tax-Free Living Strategy #2*. Certain deductions wouldn't appear to apply to you, but if you know to take them, you not only pay less in taxes, you improve your chances of sailing through the system untouched. It sounds odd, I know. But it's how the IRS's strange pretzel logic works. I've talked with dozens of revenue agents over the years. They all tell the same story:

The IRS computers are programmed to catch returns that stand out from the crowd. If you don't take every single deduction or tax break you're entitled to, or if you don't take the deductions that are standard for your type of return, you will stick out like a sore thumb. You will be flagged as either a liar, a fool or both.

The idea, then, is to take an aggressive stance . . . like the pros do . . . so that your return fits the professional patterns that don't attract attention. We make it easy to do, as you will see.

The truth about how the IRS really works.

Tax-Free Living Strategy #3 is simple: Take advantage of the little tax tricks that the Club's specialists tell you about. For instance, it's fine to pay your taxes in April but never ever file your return until August. The IRS insists that it makes no difference. But the truth is, IRS agents work on quotas which they've usually met by August. So by filing late, you tilt the scales to your advantage.

Other little tricks like this one will come in your monthly communiques and in a special briefing paper that I want to send you at no charge.

But first let me tell you about *Strategy #4*

because I know a lot about it. I work part-time at home. I conduct only part of my business from home, so I would appear to be a prime target of IRS scrutiny. But I've never heard one peep from the IRS because I take precautions.

For example, I had a photo taken of me sitting in my office, reading *The London Times*. I made sure the newspaper's date showed in the photo, then I framed the picture and hung it on my wall as proof that I work at home.

There are many more precautions and inventive strategies like this that you can't get from 99% of the CPAs, newsletters, and freebie tax booklets they hand out every April 15th. But it's the kind of advice you can expect from the Club.

JAMES

Strategy #5 is a big one, because it's the last of the great tax shelters. It allows you to invest and build wealth without ever paying a single penny in taxes—it's the ultimate in tax-free living!

This tax shelter that allows you to invest any way you like—in stocks, bonds, mutual funds, whatever you please—earning high double-digit returns that compound tax-free.

This shelter is none other than variable annuities. These used to be triple losers—mixing a complex insurance policy with measly returns and expensive fees. But that has all changed.

A number of first-rate annuity companies now offer policies that are holding high-performing stocks and bonds in their portfolios. Plus, they've cut their fees so that they're competitive with mutual funds.

Not only do you enjoy the advantages of tax deferral on your investment earnings, you get an insurance benefit to boot. A variable annuity is set up so that the cash left over will pass onto your heirs directly—avoiding the costs and headaches of probate.

What's more, this shelter allows you to sock away as much as you want. There are no ceilings like with IRAs, Keoghs, and the 401(k). Plus, if you should suddenly need your money, you can make withdrawals without paying a penalty, as long as you choose the right plan.

JOSEPH

The Club has surveyed the field of annuities and investigated each of the popular annuity companies. We have subjected them to the most rigorous testing—on paper and in actual use. We have found companies that have been around for decades, that offer you a choice of conservative or aggressive portfolios, that are managed by pros we can trust.

We also provide you with an entree to over-seas annuity programs, especially the ever pop-ular Swiss annuities. These annuities are ideal for members who wish to sock away some cash in an absolutely-safe overseas haven. Money stored in a Swiss haven cannot be attacked by lawyers, creditors, ex-wives or anybody.

Lawyers, creditors, ex-wives . . . your money is beyond their reach.

When you join the Oxford Club, you will receive regular briefings on annuities and other offshore financial strategies. You will learn all about the *Swiss Money Strategies* and the exalted world of supreme asset protection.

As you proceed, you will probably have ques-tions or want to pursue one of the recommend-ed annuities. You will again find the Club to be of invaluable assistance. Just call your *Member Services Liaison* and ask for further help. You will be given a thorough analysis of the best options so that you can make the wisest decision for your personal financial needs.

Whichever approach you take—domestic or offshore—the annuity is perfect for automatical-ly building your wealth while deferring taxes on your earnings.

WILLIAM

Taxes are the most obvious, but not the most odious, attack on your right to wealth. We'll discuss other threats in our next session.

The Oxford Portfolio Top Holdings

1994		1993		1992		1992	
Caledonia Mining	1380%	Hoffman LaRoche	104%	Hopewell Holdings	290%		
Argosy Mining	170%	Hopewell Holdings	100%	Siam Cement	140%		
Tel...			67%			Tian An	64%
Ho...			60%			Cifra	64%
Sim...			56%			Nikkei Put Warrants	53%
CB...			47%			Tecogen	46%
Nest...						Banacci	44%
Bangkok Bank	15%	Southwestern Bell	45%			New England Electric	39%
Bank Int'l Settlem'ts	12%	Royal Dutch Petrol	32%			Asia Pacific Fund	37%
Yearly Gain	192%	Yearly Gain	65.3%	Yearly Gain		Yearly Gain	86.3%

1992 Siam Cement — Oxfords go wherever in the world the profits are good. Here we capitalized on the global building boom.

Chapter Seven

A MAN'S RIGHT TO ASSET PROTECTION

Perhaps you have been putting off estate planning for, say, mañana? Well, you're going to love the "easy Oxford" approach.

JAMES

Many of us would rather talk about a stranger's prostrate than delve into the intricacies of living wills, family trusts, probate and the like. It's understandable.

The paperwork alone is enough to drive us bonkers. It's amazing to me to think that the Lord's prayer has 57 words, the Gettysburg Address has 266 words, the Ten Commandments has 297 words, the Declaration of Independence has 300 words, and the average lawyer will weigh you down with an estate document containing 25,000 words. It's a shame.

And it's one of the big reasons that so many people leave all their years of hard work to the lawyers and the government. A typical family gives away $100,000 . . . simply because they don't want to face up to estate planning.

But it doesn't have to be. The Oxford Club

has pioneered an approach to estate planning that eliminates legal hassles. This approach can be summed up in seven words.

Just seven words can mean the difference between an estate that your family appreciates or the lawyers appreciate. These seven words will make more sense after you've heard the true story of a man who almost made it to the Club too late . . .

The "Lucky Seven" solution to estate planning hassles.

Gus and Dot, those were the parents' names. They were the all-American couple: three kids, a successful bakery business, a house in the suburbs, a small portfolio of stocks and bonds, all for a net worth of about $1.2 million. The oldest son, a dashing entrepreneur himself, planned to take over the family business when the time came. It was a picture book story.

JOSEPH

Now you may be thinking, with assets of $1.2 million, this couple doesn't have much in common with many people. But the fact is, a million dollars isn't all that much anymore. Anybody with a home, business interests, and a few possessions now qualifies.

JAMES

Gus and Dot started out their estate planning just fine. They drew up an estate plan in the '70s, leaving everything to each other and eventually to the kids. It was nothing fancy, but it was better than most people do.

Things were going fine until 1982. That's when they updated their will to take advantage of a new marital deduction. They also looked into long-term care insurance, but it seemed too expensive. They had Medicare and a Medigap policy, so they decided to pass on the insurance. Finally, they transferred half the interest in the family bakery to their son—since he would be running it soon.

Everything continued along until 1992 when Gus suffered a fatal heart attack. That's when Dot's problems really began. She thought her estate plan was in order. They had, after all, updated the plan to take advantage of the marital deduction. That meant that Dot wouldn't now get hit with estate taxes.

JOSEPH

I should interject that the marital deduction didn't even exist until 1981. Anyone who hasn't updated their will since that time would be wise to update it immediately.

People who haven't updated their wills are in for a rude awakening.

JAMES

Unfortunately, though they had updated their will, they left out a crucial clause—*the credit shelter clause.* It may sound like legalese, but it's easy to understand. It simply means that $600,000 of your estate goes into a trust that is completely exempt from estate taxes. This little mistake would cost the family $192,800 in taxes down the road. But the family had more immediate problems facing them.

Six months after Gus died, Dot had to go into a nursing home. Because she had inherited all of Gus' assets, she was ineligible for any Medicaid assistance. The last year of Dot's life cost the family $96,000 for care that should have cost nothing.

The family should have invested a few thousand dollars in an insurance policy that guaranteed adequate nursing home care.

A nursing home shouldn't drain the family fortune.

With nursing homes costing upwards of $8,000 a month these days, an insurance policy is a "must have." Since so many people are facing this difficult issue today, the Oxford Club provides timely information on the best options and strategies in our regular communiques.

The family's problems continued to mount. Most of their assets had been tied up in real estate and in the stock of their bakery. That was a serious mistake.

If they had followed the Club's advice to transfer their assets to the children in a systematic way while they were still alive, things would have gone better.

But as it was, the son had to sell the building the bakery was located in. It was a distress sale, because he had to raise $192,800 practically overnight to pay the estate taxes. He is now renting space, and his fragile business could easily go under.

Adding insult to injury, the children were forced into probate because Gus and Dot hadn't taken the one easy step to avoid the expense and hassle of probate. Subsequent lawyers fees cost the family another 7% of the estate's value.

Add it all up—taxes, the nursing home, the distress sale, and probate costs—the estate of $1.2 million was cut to $800,000 in a few short months. It was at this point that the son joined the Club . . .

Right away, he learned that the family could

have avoided almost all of the hassles and the lost
cash with one simple step. All they had to do
was form a simple *Living Trust* or a *Family Limited Partnership*. There are also overseas trust
plans that aren't much more difficult to set up
but which can build an even stronger shield
around your wealth for generations to come.

The nest egg was nearly
fried in a hot skillet.

It was too late for the son to undo the mis-
takes of the past, but not too late to plan more
wisely for the future. The Club assured him that
he would be in good company from here on out.
All he had to do was remember seven magical
words:

TRUST THE RESOURCES
OF THE OXFORD CLUB.

That's all you need to do, too. The Club
introduces you to the world's finest (and nicest)
attorneys—pros who can make sense of estate
planning. In the private communiques, at the
chapter meetings, and at the annual soirees, these
top attorneys can put together problem-proof
strategies for you.

JOSEPH

You might be wondering how the Club can afford all this high priced legal talent. It's the same way we afford everything else. It's based on the network concept, the buddy system.

We attract the top attorneys because by joining, they too are made privy to a world beyond their own expertise. They too get the inside line on our international stock plays, overseas banking secrets, tax strategies, and so much more.

WILLIAM

It's the idea of "good profits in the company of good men." And to take you to the next step of this idea, we have assembled another briefing paper for you.

It's titled *Asset Protection Made Easy*. It will insure that your wealth remains in your family where it belongs.

To receive this special briefing, please turn to page 125. Or to learn about the most insidious threat facing you as an American today, turn the page.

THE OXFORD PORTFOLIO TOP HOLDINGS

1994		1993		1992
Caledonia Mining	1380%	Hoffman LaRoche	104%	
Argosy Mining	170%	Hopewell Holdings	100%	
Telebras	49%	Bank Int'l Settlem'ts	77%	
Holderbank	32%	Singapore Airlines	67%	
Singapore Airlines	28%	Thai Capital Fund	60%	
CEPA	24%	Latin Amer. Inv. Fund	56%	
Nestle	18%	Siemens	47%	
Bangkok Bank	15%	Southwestern Bell	%	
Bank Int'l Settlem'ts	12%	Royal Dutch Petrol	32%	
Yearly Gain 192%		**Yearly Gain** 65.3%		**Yearly Gain** 86.3%

> **1993 ROYAL DUTCH PETROLEUM** — This 32% gainer is as safe as stock investing gets—but it still performed three times better than the U.S. market averages.

Chapter Eight

A MAN'S RIGHT TO COMPLETE PRIVACY

*In the Land of the Lawyers, it's You vs.
The Snivelers, Slackers and One Million
Lawyers In Their Employ.*

JAMES

There was a time when people had very clear ideas about legal and illegal, moral and immoral, honorable and dishonorable. Ideas based on the Bible and Greek concepts of virtue. Ideas that endured well into the 20th century . . . when something happened.

All of a sudden, everything that had been considered virtuous was now considered naive and narrow-minded. Everything that had been immoral and deviant was now something to be tolerated and protected. What brought this on? Where did America go wrong?

I look out across America, the country I love, and can't help but hang my head in disgust.

I see doctors who used to pay $10,000 a year for malpractice insurance now paying $100,000. Half the country's OB-GYNs have stopped delivering babies because they can't show a profit. More malpractice suits were filed in the last decade than in the entire history of American tort law. Are today's doctors that bad, or has something gone terribly wrong?

I look out across America and see policemen spending most their day doing paperwork for the courtroom. Have our streets gotten any safer for it? Is there any less wrongdoing?

I see the courtrooms so backlogged from lawyers' never-ending motions and pleadings and stalling techniques that nobody takes a court decision seriously. And no justice is done. Hell, crime's never been worse. Law-abiding citizens are afraid to leave their homes at night!

I see my grandchild in the Boy Scouts, and my heart aches for him. His Troop can't even host a baseball game in the city park anymore because they can't afford the liability insurance. Something is terribly wrong with this.

Something is happening to the fabric of America.

We are witnessing a steady unraveling of the beliefs and ethics that made this country great. It's a sad commentary, I know. But who can look out upon America and doubt it?

The bottom line is, the scales of justice are

out of whack. There's so many lawyers, there's no room for justice. The sue-happy and the lawyers are the winners. The hard workers, the inventors, the entrepreneurs, we are the losers. We are the chief targets of the snivelers, slackers, and one million lawyers in their employ. If you haven't already been sued, you will be.

You have no choice but to take defensive measures. You must protect your loved ones from the onslaught. You need a program to shield your assets and your life's work. You must ensure your right to privacy . . . and the Oxford Club can be your first line of defense.

Meet the unlawyers—men who undo other lawyers' damage.

JOSEPH

The Club has assembled a remarkable brain-trust of *un*lawyers—a remarkable breed of lawyer who specializes in undoing what other lawyers have fouled up. We count among our ranks some of the most refreshing names in civil law. Men of intellect. Men who'll gladly beat up on the two-bit lawyers that sully late night TV.

WILLIAM

As you may have guessed, we feel passionately about the state of the law, and about the myriad threats to our privacy. We are angered by the sharp increase in threats to our Members' privacy and personal security.

Here's a story of a very different kind that almost incited me to riot the first time I heard it.

A couple was returning home from a vacation in Maui. As they drove up to their home, their neighbors were watching them with guarded expressions. Yellow neon police tape was wrapped around their property line and chains blocked their front door. Two men were seated in an unmarked car, the morning sun reflecting off their sunglasses.

Sounds like a made-for-TV movie, but it's real life.

What had the couple done wrong? They had no idea! All they were able to ascertain in the weeks and months that followed . . . was that their bank had sold their home mortgage contract to another bank which had then accused them of falsifying their income on their original mortgage application five years back.

No evidence was ever presented against them.

The Marshals just swooped in with RICO papers and padlocked their house. It was seized for something as simple as having filled out their mortgage application the wrong way.

JOSEPH

This is not an isolated story. It has become a dangerous world for law-abiding citizens. Affronts to our privacy have escalated 500% in seven years. An Oxford Club Member who is a private investigator recently told us about an Orwellian nightmare he uncovered.

He used the Freedom of Information Act to find out that Big Brother is now using computers to cross-match mortgage applications with tax returns. That's right! They're hoping to find properties that are candidates for forfeiture.

WILLIAM

It's not just mortgage applications.

There are now more than 100 offenses for which federal, state, or local governments can seize your property. They don't even have to indict you. A recent Pittsburgh Press survey found that 80% of the civil forfeitures are not— I repeat, not accompanied by an arrest!

Did you know that if you go fishing on the wrong rivers in Florida, the police can confiscate your boat, trailer, and even your car? Yes, just for fishing!

Or if they don't like your religious views, or think you're evading taxes, or suspect you of insider trading, or don't like the people you associate with, or, or, or—the list gets longer every year. There may not even be probable cause that you've done something wrong.

When you add in all the attacks on personal privacy from all the levels of government, the people's right "to be secure in their persons, houses, papers and effects against unreasonable searches and seizures" has become a joke.

Which leads to the question, Where is it all headed?

Why is the Fed doing this to innocent people?

How long will it be before the government is setting up roadblocks at random points across the country . . . applying RICO to anything they don't like? How dangerous will our world become?

JAMES

Nobody knows. We know only that in the future, a man can't be too private about his affairs. That's why we have assembled another very special briefing paper for you. The briefing uses information that a private investigator keyed us into. Information you can use to create a lawsuit-proof, snoop-proof, bullet-proof protection program for your assets and your family's privacy.

The briefing is titled *Personal and Financial Security in a Dangerous World* and it's yet another gift that you will receive immediately upon acceptance as an Oxford Club member. Perhaps now is the time to join…before one of the threats hits home.

THE OXFORD PORTFOLIO TOP HOLDINGS

1994		1993		1992	
Caledonia Mining	1380%	Hoffman LaRoche	104%	Hopewell Holdings	290%
Argosy Mining	170%	Hopewell Holdings	100%	Siam Cement	140%
Telebras	49%	Bank Int'l Settlem'ts	?%	Asia Pacific Fund	?%
Holderbank	32%	Singapore Airlines	67%		
Singapore Airlines	28%	Thai Capital Fund	60%		
CEPA	24%	Latin Amer. Inv. Fund	56%		
Nestle	18%	Siemans	47%		
Bangkok Bank	15%	Southwestern Bell	45%		
Bank Int'l Settlem'ts	12%	Royal Dutch Petrol	32%		
Yearly Gain	**192%**	**Yearly Gain**	**65.3%**	**Yearly Gain**	**86.3%**

> **1993 HOPEWELL HOLDINGS (HONG KONG)** — We capitalized on China's big boom with this pick, bringing home 390% profits since 1989.

Chapter Nine

A MAN'S RIGHT TO SAFE HARBOR

Get your money out of your country before your country gets it out of you. This "turnkey approach" makes it elementary.

JAMES

I began this briefing by saying that I love America. It was not empty flag waving.

In my lifetime, I have seen America's people survive a Great Depression that toppled most of the world's governments.

We've come back from Pearl Harbor to win the greatest military victory in modern history.

We've gone from the horse and buggy to putting men on the moon and bringing them safely home.

Today's living Americans have fought harder, paid a higher price for freedom, and done more to advance the dignity of man than any people who ever lived. We are an amazing people.

And the way I see it, we can be trusted to make our own decisions about what's best for our families. We can be trusted with a greater share of our earnings. And we don't need some bean counter telling us how to order our affairs.

We hold with the Founding Fathers and Jimmy Durante.

We believe that government is the servant, not the master; that it was meant to maintain order and protect our safety. But otherwise, in the words of that noted political philosopher, Jimmy Durante, "Don't put no constrictions on da people, leave 'em da heck alone."

That's our philosophy, and we proudly stand by it.

But by the same token, we never allow ourselves to become complacent or foolhardy. We know that we face numerous threats from lawyers run amuck, from an IRS hellbent on bleeding us like turnips, from a government of drunken sailors on liberty.

We have been shown the folly of not having at least one year's living expenses socked away in a safe overseas bank account.

WILLIAM

But let's be frank. Most people get nervous about sending money to an offshore bank whose name they can barely pronounce. I know I felt that way 20 years ago, before the Oxford Club.

JAMES

It's healthy to be nervous. There are all sorts of overseas programs being offered today; some of them are first rate, some are downright dangerous. But it doesn't matter how good an overseas program is if you don't understand it. It's best to venture overseas slowly, cautiously, using the Oxford Club's "turnkey" approach. Let's examine it:

You start with an objective—that is, to set up a simple bank account in a friendly country like Canada or Switzerland.

You will want an account that's safe, liquid, flexible, where you can get personal attention if you need it. You have to feel completely comfortable—that's the overriding issue. And comfort comes from familiarity, from knowing that your bank is always going to be there. Always.

A bank is no better than its management. For this reason, I have long been impressed with Geneva's Banque Union de Credit. It proved its mettle in my book a few years ago.

Its director, Camille Perusett, did something no normal banker would do: He paid out 150 million Swiss francs to depositors in a single day, as a result of a mistaken bank run. He did it with ease—demonstrating very clearly that he runs a fully liquid bank. No American bank could have done that.

A level of safety you'd
never even hope for in
an American bank.

In addition to safety, I also look for flexibility and ease of contact. An overseas bank should be willing to bend over backwards to help you preserve and increase your wealth.

It should be able to buy every stock, bond, currency, and precious metal traded anywhere on earth. And you should always be able to deal with top management. The idea of the Swiss banker being aloof and unapproachable is hogwash. If you have money on deposit in the right bank, they will make time for you.

JAMES

Having said that . . . which banks can you recommend as a safe haven for a new Member?

WILLIAM

There are three or four banks in Switzerland and Canada that have a history of treating Members right.

New members looking to store away $20,000 as a warm-up ought to take a close look at Geneva-based Banque Union de Credit. It has been around forever, it's plenty big without appearing to be so, and its staff is first rate. Director

Camille Perusett has been in charge since 1971 and is always accessible, welcoming your every question.

He meets often with Club Members and takes the time to explain how recent changes in Swiss banking policy have cut the costs and fees of banking—making it cheaper than it was a decade ago.

He can show you how to structure your account properly so that you pay no Swiss taxes. Or if you like, you can once again trust the resources of the Club. You can have your *Member Services Liaison* handle all the nitty-gritty for you.

JOSEPH

It's that kind of personalized attention that I value. I had expected all kinds of hurdles when I first tried to open an overseas bank account. But I had it all wrong. It was no harder than opening a credit card account—especially when you have your Club liaison guiding you through the process.

WILLIAM

You'll find that to open an account at Perusett's bank or at the bank of your choice, you simply contact the bank by phone or fax and ask for account opening papers. Or to make it easier, the Club can handle it. We've set up a turnkey program with many of the world's safest banks ... so we can assist your every step ... beginning by faxing your name and address to the bank so they can easily forward the account application papers to you.

That's the kind of simplicity that makes a Club valuable!

You next fill out the forms and send them to the bank. A week or so later, you have your own private account that nobody but you knows about. Then, when it comes time to depositing some money in your new account, it's just as easy.

You do it through a correspondent bank. All foreign banks have correspondent banks in the U.S. where they hold accounts. Just ask your bank for a list of its correspondent banks in the U.S. Choose one you know and trust, then instruct your local bank or broker to wire your money to the correspondent bank.

In actuality, your money never leaves the country. But for all legal intents and purposes, it's safely overseas.

Plus, it's totally private because banks don't report interbank wire transfers. They couldn't even report them if Uncle Sam wanted them too. Trillions of dollars are wired every day—it's too much to follow. I've wired millions over the years and there has never been a paper trail of any kind. It's all very easy and very private.

This level of easy international banking has kept me solvent through business failures, through a divorce, through more than one frivolous lawsuit. Without this protection, I would have been destroyed.

JAMES

You too would be wise to strive for this level of asset protection. It is the final step you will take to secure your right to wealth.

Privacy. Prosperity. Tradition.
That's the Oxford Club.

We have taken the time to offer you this private briefing because we believe you will find common cause in our Club. We believe that you are looking for breakthrough investments… asset protection strategies…the comraderie of good men making good money…the potential for exciting new business alliances…the tools you need to master every situation and prosper on a grand scale. If indeed this is what you're looking for, then you can rest assured that it's all in the Club.

As a new Member, you will receive the first of 12 confidential communiques, a Membership passcard, a list of upcoming Club activities, the Club's hotline phone number, an update of our investment portfolio, plus four valuable briefing papers.

Each month you will receive additional benefits in the form of urgent investment bulletins, invitations to regional Chapter meetings, luxury pleasure weekends, global profit expeditions and so much more.

Yes, there is a whole new world awaiting you.

JOSEPH

It's a world in which good men are making good money, watching out for one another, mindful of each other's health and well being. A world in which nobody questions a man's right to wealth.

If I could borrow from the great Steve Allen...my friend, this could be the start of something big! To find out for sure if the Oxford Club is for you, you would do well to hear from some of our Members. These are men who've moved their investments onto solid ground . . . and made the most of their portfolios . . . while vowing to never again accept a loss gracefully.

Each of these men has his own story to tell:

$10,000 IN TWO WEEKS

"I want to tell you about my experience with the

Oxford Club's recommendation to open an account at the Union Bank of Credit in Geneva. It was great to be able to talk directly to manager Camille Perusset—I've done so three times so far. Getting money over there was easy. I got the wire transfer number at Chase Manhattan Bank and it was over there in a jiffy. We put it all in Swiss franc judiciary deposits. What a great move! I received the report the other day: I've made $10,000 in just two weeks by being in a safe cash instrument."

Andrew W., Houston, TX

INVALUABLE CONTACTS

"I cannot afford not to be a Member. My company has been very successful this year, thanks to a financing contact I made through the Club's Member Information Exchange."

Douglas K., Topeka, KS

DETAILED EXPLANATIONS

"I am quite frankly impressed. Yours is the only newsletter I have ever received where the editor explains how to actually go about making an investment."   **Randolph C., Edmond, OK**

$17,000 IN ONE YEAR

"I've made a lot of money from your recommendations. The two I've most benefitted from was...Hopewell Holdings—I pocketed over $17,000 in one year in profits, and your sell on Japanese stocks two years ago."

Cliff M., Redding, CA

A GLOBAL NETWORK
"Through a Member I was introduced to in Austria, I found a wonderful job. The Oxford Club has changed my life."

Wolfgang N., Dusseldorf, Germany

INVESTOR'S ADVOCATE
"You are a real fighter for the rights and benefits of individual and private concerns."

James D., Pinellas Park, FL

RESEARCH ASSISTANCE
"I have been a Member for several years and one of the reasons I continue to extend my Membership is directly credited to the efficient and expeditious manner in which the staff handles my special requests for research and information."

Steven G., Kuala Lumpur, Malaysia

FRIENDS AND CONTACTS
"We've been able to develop a number of fine friends and valuable business contacts."

Richard L., Palm Beach, FL

PERSONAL ASSISTANCE
"Dear Research Department: You have always answered my questions in simple terms and given the needed information. It's a pleasure to work with you."   **W.C.D., Louisville, KY**

GLOBAL PROFIT TAKING
"I've made lots of money on your Latin America investment picks...thank you."

Roger B., Costa Mesa, CA

PROFITABLE INVESTMENT TOURS
"You do a tremendous job arranging investment tours. They provide a unique perspective and are always informative and provide valuable contacts. We have profited nicely."

Wallace E., New York, NY

The Oxford Club maintains strict privacy for its Members. We do not rent or sell Members' names to outside organizations and we will not use their last names in any written materials. We promise you that the members quoted in this report are real people. In fact, it is quite possible that you might be sitting next to them at the next Oxford Club meeting!

The Oxford Club isn't for everyone. If it is for you, then the best is still to come. Turn to Appendix A.

Appendix A: THE OXFORD CLUB PORTFOLIO TOP HOLDINGS 1991-1994

1994

Caledonia Mining	1380%	Argosy Mining	170%
Telebras	49%	Holderbank	32%
Singapore Airlines	28%	CEPA	24%
Bangkok Bank	15%	Bank Int'l Settlements	12%
Royal Dutch Petrol	11%	**Yearly Gain**	**192%**

1993

Hoffman La Roche	104%	Hopewell Holdings	100%
Bank Int'l Settlements	77%	Singapore Airlines	67%
Thai Capital Fund	60%	Latin Amer. Inv. Fund	56%
Siemans	47%	Southwestern Bell	45%
Royal Dutch Petrol	32%	**Yearly Gain**	**65.3%**

1992

Hopewell Holdings	290%	Siam Cement	140%
Tian An	64%	Cifra	64%
Nikkei Put Warrants	53%	Tecogen	46%
Banacci	44%	New England Electric	39%
Asia Pacific Fund	37%	**Yearly Gain**	**86.3%**

1991

Kaiser Steel	160%	Tian An	94%
Response Technology	88%	HSBC Holdings	83%
Telefonos de Mexico	66%	Brazil Fund	65%
Chile Fund	55%	Latin Amer. Inv. Fund	40%
Illinois Power	31%	**Yearly Gain**	**75.8%**

Appendix B: **A GILDED ROLODEX**

Imagine walking into a corner market in one of the world's classiest neighborhoods and taking a look at the bulletin board. All kinds of listings would be posted. A whole new world of opportunities would open up to you.

Well, imagine no more. As an Oxford Club Member, you will have access to our monthly bulletin board, allowing you to tap into a global network of exclusive contacts. You can submit your own personal or business announcements free of charge. Below are some recent announcements.

Note: We have edited these listings to protect Members' identities and to quickly communicate the essence of the offer.

FINANCING AVAILABLE — Offering $50,000 and up for new/existing businesses, commercial real estate. Low fees and fast, professional service.

TRAVEL COMPANION — Bilingual European lady seeks to serve as a travel companion in exchange for expenses.

IMPORT/EXPORT CONTACT — Importer is interested in communicating with other Members in the business to establish mutually beneficial relationships.

FREE ADVERTISING — Members may advertise in

any one of three widely-distributed and well-read international sales/marketing directories.

COCKTAIL PARTY — For our Oxford Club friends in the Philadelphia area, we're hosting a social gathering at our home.

SCHOLARSHIP MONEY — Member has a proprietary database of 200,000 scholarship money sources. Will tailor to your student's needs/desires.

TRAVEL LOVERS — Save money and earn commissions on every trip you take. This is not a travel club; it's an offer to Oxford Club Members only.

INVEST IN A MOTION PICTURE — Have you ever dreamed of investing in, helping to produce, even playing a bit part in a major film? Call us!

A "HEALTH FOR LIFE" PROGRAM — Members receive a 15% discount at a state-of-the-art health and rejuvenation spa near Cancun.

Whether you have property for sale, need venture capital, want a travel companion, or whatever your desire—you will find a 'gilded rolodex' on Page 11 of each Oxford Club communique.

*What can you expect in your first year
as an Oxford Club Member? Read on.*

Appendix C: 119 LEVELS OF WEALTH AND WELL BEING

As an Oxford Club Member, you will prosper in so many ways—in your outlook on the world, in your approach to travel, in the wealth you obtain and learn to safeguard.

Here is a summary of the 119 levels of wealth and well being that will come your way in the months and years ahead.

1. You will enjoy good profits in the company of good men.

2. You will be the first into stocks like Caledonia Mining—up 1,540% in its first year.

3. You will probably become a millionaire (if you aren't now).

4. You won't give a hoot about who's running the show in Washington—you'll be sitting pretty above it all.

5. You may not learn to read a balance sheet, but that's okay. The Club's experts will do it for you.

6-9. You will be better adapted to today's markets through a **3-phase power strategy**.

10. Your money will be invested in the world's safest havens, whether it's Canton, Ohio or Canton, China.

11. You'll experience the **predictive genius** of the S-curves.

12. You'll spend hours with the Club Directory, planning ventures with fellow Members.

13-22. You will pick up ten strategies for living tax-free right away.

23-28. You'll have an opportunity to profit from six **breakthrough blue chips** of tomorrow.

29. You will say *sayonara* to incompetent lawyers— you will be judgement proof, your assets impenetrable, your good name untouchable.

30-34. At least five astoundingly **lucrative real estate** deals will be offered in the coming year.

35. You will turn your broker from an enemy to an ally (which is better than outright despising him, anyway).

36. Your family fortune will be safe from all the money-grubbers who covet it.

37. You will receive no-nonsense Research Briefings when you join, and again throughout the year.

38-41. You will learn four strategies for **taking profits**; in fact, you will spend considerable time taking profits.

42. You will set up asset protection plans without the legal hassles.

43-49. You just might find yourself retiring to Belize or one of seven other overseas Edens that the Oxford Club has scoped out for Members exclusively!

50. Unless you request otherwise, you can count on being contacted from time to time by fellow Members with **business propositions.**

51-52. You will learn two ingenious plans (used by high rollers around the world) to borrow money privately.

53-54. You may open up a super-private Swiss or Canadian bank account (it takes about 30 minutes).

55. You will have a **consumer advocate** on your side, steering you clear of scams and fraudulent schemes.

56. You may obtain an offshore credit card that you can use to make purchases of up to $10,000 without reporting it to the IRS.

57. You will be among an elite few who recognize and profit from the emerging trends of 1996, 1997, 1998, well, you get the idea.

58-61. You will learn about four great **sideline**

businesses that are perfect for a housewife or a "semi-retired" couple.

62. You will receive free special reports such as the Insider's Guide to Fine Art Collecting.

63-67. You will never again be caught off-guard by the five retirement wreckers.

68. You will **travel creatively**, and with ambition. Your every weekend jaunt could become a tax-free business junket.

69-78. You'll be given ten sure-fire tips and insider sources to help you raise venture capital.

79. You will hook into a clearinghouse of **new inventions** and business ideas.

80. You will learn about offshore maildrops, and how they could save your business from legal disaster.

81. You will meet so many successful investors that winning habits will rub off.

82. You will learn how to profit from the world's emerging markets.

83. You will pay far less in taxes. Far less.

84. You will see your business grow in leaps and bounds when you begin using the Club's

extraordinary **referral sources.**

85. You will learn to distinguish between "raw information" and "actionable knowledge."

86. You will feel more secure knowing that your financial affairs are being conducted in complete privacy.

87. Whatever your financial interests—stocks, bonds, real estate, commodities, precious metals, you will have a *Member Services Liaison* to help you make wise moves.

88. You will receive an annual survey of precious-metals dealers—insuring the highest quality at the lowest price.

89. Our man behind the Cuban curtain will bring you travel and investment opportunities aplenty.

90. You will never again sweat the complicated insurance game.

91. If you've refinanced your home recently, you will use this **valuable deduction** that 96% of all CPAs don't apply.

92. You will be invited to Oxford University for advanced tutelage.

93. You will be updated on pension plan problems—so you won't fall victim.

94-99. You will learn the six key steps to take in any dangerous situation to protect yourself and your loved ones.

100. You will get the inside line on auction news, wine purchases and other fine aspects of good living.

101. Your "safe money" will be earning **100%-200% more** than CDs.

102. You will develop critical insights into current political affairs.

103. You will become less reliant on slow-poke U.S. news sources so that your foreign holdings are always safe and sound.

104. You will cut your chances of facing a tax audit dramatically.

105. You will learn how your company can be used to deduct all of your personal medical bills.

106-115. The ten top Swiss Money Strategies will become second nature to you.

116. You will enjoy substantial Member discounts in your travels.

117. You will turn your hobby into a grand-slam enterprise—a tax-deductible, profit-

generating, rollicking good time.

118. You'll step up to a tax-free lifestyle.

119. And lastly, you will be joining a Club that's good enough for you. Welcome!

There you have it, 119 levels of wealth and well being. We chose the number 119 for good reason. It is intended to show you how remarkably profitable the Oxford Club can be for you:

You see, during this trial nominating period, the Club's Annual Dues of $150 are being waived and you need only pay the Club's Trial Fee of $119. Each of the above benefits is yours, then, for $1 apiece. We can't imagine a better deal. So go ahead and choose the course of your future.

This Could Be The Start of Something Big!

Appendix D

BENEFITS OF OXFORD CLUB MEMBERSHIP

Monthly Communiques *(Value: $150)*

Your first monthly communique may surprise you. This 12-page gem is not *crammed* with advice. It contains only one or two astoundingly profitable strategies, explained in painstaking detail so you have *everything* you need to make a safe, intelligent decision. With your first communique, you will also receive our current investment portfolio, our by-laws, rules on privacy, personal passcard, and more . . .

The Exclusive Oxford Club Library *(Value: $125)*

The Club maintains a world-class library of Executive Briefings on a myriad of subjects. You will automatically receive our four most popular papers to introduce you to the finest wealth-building strategies available today.

Urgent Investment Bulletins *(Value: $75)*

The global markets never sleep. If your investments are about to light up, or burn out, you want to know beforehand. Or if our agents uncover a hot opportunity, you want in before the crowd. We make it happen by rushing you an express mail message. It will be short and sweet, preparing you to take decisive action.

Member Services Liaison *(Value: $250)*

When the communiques and executive briefings aren't enough, you have an entire research department to access. These pros can answer just about any question or fill any request. They can help you open an overseas bank account, make a business contact, run a computer search—you name it. Your own research team is only a phone call away.

Confidential Telephone Alert *(Value: $100)*

Communiques, briefings, personal assistance, what more can we do for our Members? Plenty! Members are given a confidential phone number to call—at any time—to receive critical advice on the status of the markets and the Club's investment portfolio.

Annual Gala Reception *(Invaluable)*

This black-tie optional party is your official welcome to the Oxford Club, and every year it gets better. You never know what Membership Director Julia Guth is planning. Only one thing is certain. You will meet extraordinary people, make lasting friendships, and take home fond memories and valuable business cards.

PROFITEERING EXPEDITIONS *(Invaluable)*

The take-charge spirit of the Oxford Club's founders is abundantly alive in our global financial tours. The aim is to have a rollicking good time *and* to come back with the goods. On the latest trip to Belize, we uncovered prime investment property and cut business deals. Where will the Club go next? Wherever the world's biggest profits await!

COMMISSION-FREE INVESTING *(Value: $150-$1,000)*

The country's leading international brokerage has made an exclusive offer to Oxford Club Members: Trade any NYSE or AMEX stock (up to a $250,000 trade) and pay nothing. Or you can buy an international stock, receive the best advice money can buy, and still get your U.S. stock trade—free of charge! This guaranteed $150 to $1,000 savings is reason enough to join the Club—though it's hardly the only reason . . .

THE PRIZED BLUE BOOK *(Value: Unlimited)*

This 180-page directory is a virtual "Who's Who" of 20th Century talent. You'll find the "vitals" on the financial wizards of our time, as well as artists, academics, and businessmen in nearly every field of endeavor. Yes, this is the

Members' roster (and Members who wish to be included must submit a permission form). Men have been known to join the Club merely to get their hands on "the blue book." We trust that your motives are more pure.

OXFORD STUDY FELLOWSHIP *(Invaluable)*

Where better to further your education than at the world's center of higher education, Oxford University? Members gather with a distinguished post-graduate faculty for four days of instruction and private consultation in Advanced Wealth Protection. A tour through Old England makes an enchanting complement to the program.

COMPLIMENTARY DREAM VACATION *(Value: $4,000)*

Once a year we hold a drawing for a dream weekend vacation—an all-expenses paid stay at a favorite golf resort! Perhaps it will be the PGA National in Palm Beach, or the Bing Crosby Pro/Am in Carmel. You are automatically entered to win!

MEMBER OPPORTUNITY EXCHANGE *(Value: $100)*

Insiders know it as "Page 11." It's the page of the communique that is set aside for Member use. It's your chance to make a personal announcement, offer a valuable service, ask for a travel buddy, whatever your heart's desire. Page 11 may be the most exclusive "bulletin board" in the world. And now you can use it to uncover a goldmine of contacts and opportunities you simply cannot find anywhere else.

REGIONAL CHAPTER ACTIVITIES *(Value: $300-$1,000)*

Making friends and business contacts with Club Members in your area is only half the reason to attend. You can also meet with the world's top investment, legal, and tax experts in the convenience of your hometown area. Seminars like these normally cost $295 to $995, but they are yet another benefit of Membership.

SPECIAL MEMBERS-ONLY DISCOUNTS *(Value: $50-$500)*

Because our Members are such an elite breed, a lot of companies ask for our mailing list. They don't get it. We don't take a financial interest in any products, and we don't sell our Member List. However, if a reputable company (such as a mutual fund) wishes to offer a discount to our Members, we accept it for your benefit. Or, if we negotiate a discount on a valuable product which we can endorse 100%, we will send you the information ourselves.

And oh how you benefit!
So, join the Oxford Club today.

(For new Members only)

Yes I am looking for good profits in the company of good men and gladly accept your invitation for a One-Year Trial Membership in the Oxford Club. I understand that I will receive the benefits and the guarantee outlined on the back of this form.

Your Pledge to the Oxford Club:

(please initial)

_____ I will always hold myself in a manner consistent with the club's distinguished ideals.

_____ All communications are understood to be in confidence.

_____ After the knowledge I receive brings me a net profit of at least $25,000, I'll contribute my ideas and advice.

Your Sponsor's Name __James Boxley Cooke__

Applicant's Signature _____ Date_____

Regular Annual Dues $~~150~~   waived

Trial Membership $119

❏ A check is enclosed payable to The Oxford Club
❏ Please charge: ❏ Visa ❏ MasterCard ❏ Amex

Card No_____Expires_____

Name_____

Address_____

City, State, Zip_____

THE OXFORD CLUB, U.S.A. Membership Office
105 West Monument Street, Baltimore, MD 21201

> *For Fastest Service*
> **fax to: 410-223-2640**

R119

As a New Member, You Will Receive:

✔ New Member Dossier

Includes your first communique, Membership passcard, by-laws, hotline phone number, the Club's investment portfolio, plus five research reports: *The Breakthrough Blue Chips of Tomorrow; Asset Protection Made Easy; Personal and Financial Security in a Dangerous World;* and *Ultracash: The Safety of CDs, 500% Better Returns.*

✔ Additional Benefits

You will also receive urgent investment bulletins and have an opportunity to join us in regional Chapter meetings, annual soirees, profiteering expeditions, and much more.

✔ Gentlemen's Agreement

If for any reason you're not 100% overjoyed with the profits you're taking, and you haven't prospered on a grand scale, then simply cancel for a 100% pro rata refund. Fair's fair.

(For new Members only)

Yes I am looking for good profits in the company of good men and gladly accept your invitation for a One-Year Trial Membership in the Oxford Club. I understand that I will receive the benefits and the guarantee outlined on the back of this form.

Your Pledge to the Oxford Club:

(please initial)

_____ I will always hold myself in a manner consistent with the club's distinguished ideals.

_____ All communications are understood to be in confidence.

_____ After the knowledge I receive brings me a net profit of at least $25,000, I'll contribute my ideas and advice.

Your Sponsor's Name __James Boxley Cooke__

Applicant's Signature_____ Date_____

Regular Annual Dues ~~$150~~   waived
Trial Membership $119

❏ A check is enclosed payable to The Oxford Club
❏ Please charge: ❏ Visa ❏ MasterCard ❏ Amex

Card No_____Expires_____

Name_____

Address_____

City,State, Zip_____

THE OXFORD CLUB, U.S.A. Membership Office
105 West Monument Street, Baltimore, MD 21201

For Fastest Service
fax to: 410-223-2640

R119

As a New Member, You Will Receive:

✔ New Member Dossier

Includes your first communique, Membership passcard, by-laws, hotline phone number, the Club's investment portfolio, plus five research reports: *The Breakthrough Blue Chips of Tomorrow; Asset Protection Made Easy; Personal and Financial Security in a Dangerous World;* and *Ultracash: The Safety of CDs, 500% Better Returns.*

✔ Additional Benefits

You will also receive urgent investment bulletins and have an opportunity to join us in regional Chapter meetings, annual soirees, profiteering expeditions, and much more.

✔ Gentlemen's Agreement

If for any reason you're not 100% overjoyed with the profits you're taking, and you haven't prospered on a grand scale, then simply cancel for a 100% pro rata refund. Fair's fair.